STATE SHAPES

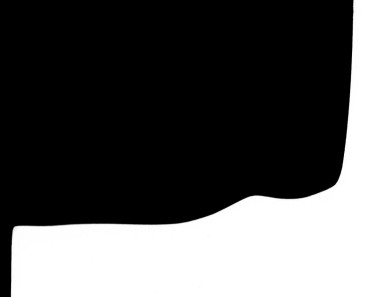

Text copyright © 2001 by Black Dog & Leventhal Publishers, Inc.
Illustrations copyright © 2001 by Rick Peterson

Published by
Black Dog & Leventhal Publishers, Inc.
151 West 19th Street
New York, NY 10011

Distributed by
Workman Publishing Company
225 Varick Street
New York, NY 10014

Designed by 27.12 design, ltd.

Manufactured in China

n m l k

Library-of-Congress Cataloging-in-Publication Data

Bruun, Erik A., 1961-
Texas / by Erik Bruun.
p. cm. -- (State Shapes)

Summary: Presents the history, important people, and famous places of the Lone Star State, as well as miscellaneous facts about Texas today.

ISBN-13: 978-1-57912-102-0

1. Texas--Juvenile literature. [1. Texas.] I. Title.

F386.3 .B78 2000

976.4--dc21   00-024671

TEXAS

By Erik Bruun

illustrated by

Rick Peterson

BLACK DOG
& LEVENTHAL
PUBLISHERS
NEW YORK

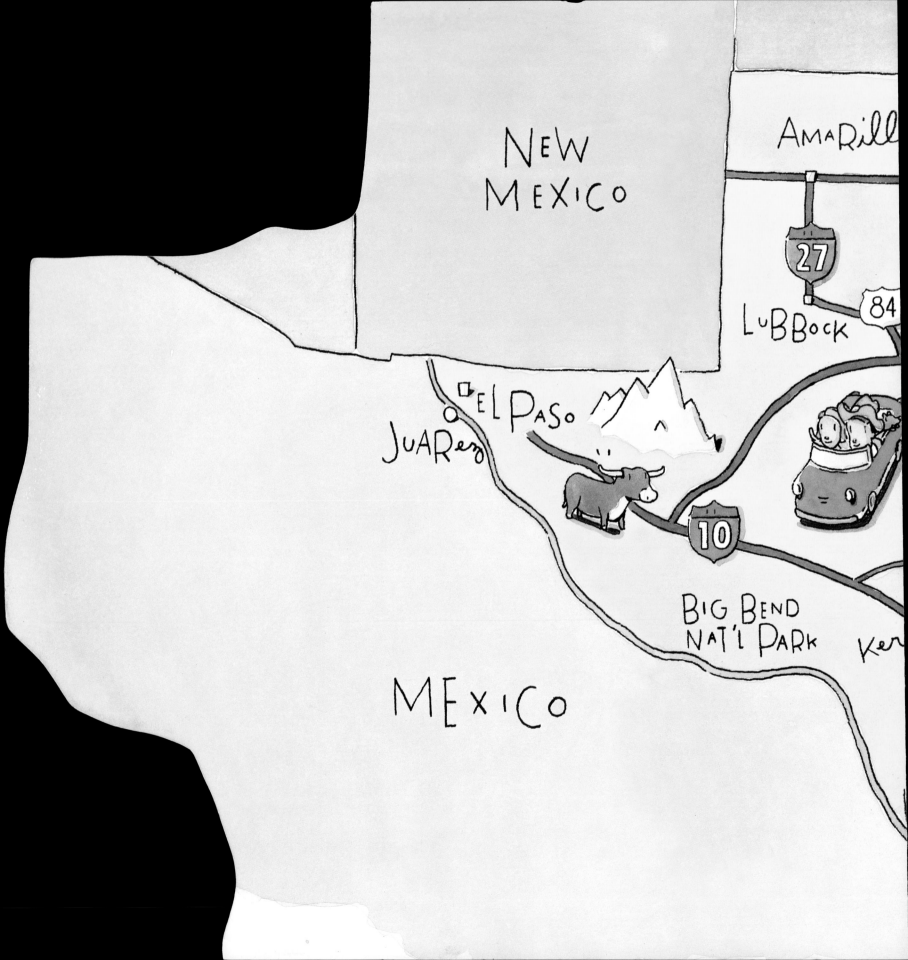

Yeeeeeee-HAW! Welcome to Texas! My name is Samuel Austin Cartwright, but you can call me Tex. I will be taking you on a tour through the great, great state of Texas.

Sounds terrific, Tex. My name's Merideth, and this is my dog, Rufus. What are you going to show us?

We will see Texas longhorns, Texas barbecue, Texas oil, Texas rodeos, and, best of all, the people of Texas. You are in for a special treat, Texan-style.

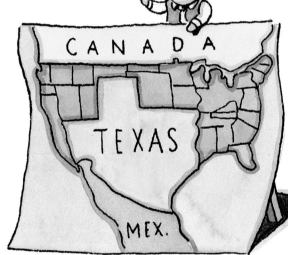

Q. What do the colors in Texas's "Lone Star" flag represent?

I can hardly wait—
        but what is Texan-style?

BIG, for starters! Everything in Texas is big. Texas is bigger than most countries—France, for one. Texas has the biggest state capitol building, the world's biggest barrier island, the biggest religious cross in the Western Hemisphere, and the biggest ranches—some bigger than the entire state of Rhode Island. We even make our rabbits big. Texan jackrabbits have the biggest rabbit ears in the world. And, of course, we have our famous ten-gallon hats.

Is that what you call that
                crazy cap on your head?

Well, bust my britches, where are my manners? I'll have to take this off for the balance of the tour. Now hold on to your hats, we'll start our journey at Texas's most sacred spot—the Alamo.

 A. Red for bravery, white for purity and blue for loyalty. The state flag pledge is: "Honor the Texas flag. I pledge allegiance to thee, Texas, one and indivisible."

Here we are at the Alamo, in San Antonio. This was the last stand of 189 heroes fighting for Texan independence.

It's beautiful. And crowded!

Three million people visit the Alamo every year, more than any other place in Texas, and rightfully so. The Alamo is famous as a Texan fort, but it was built by Spanish priests in the 1700s as a religious mission when Texas was part of Mexico. In 1836, most Texans who had moved here from the United States didn't want to stay under Mexican rule, so they declared independence. The Mexican President, Santa Anna, marched into Texas with 5,000 soldiers. A band of Texan rebels led by Jim Bowie and Colonel William Travis, which included the legendary Davy Crockett—

Q. **Why is the flag that flew over the Alamo in Mexico City's Museum of Foreign Invasions?**

The guy with the coonskin hat?

DAVY CROCKETT
KING OF THE WILD FRONTIER

Yep. He and the others holed up in the Alamo. Travis refused to surrender, declaring "victory or death," which was pretty brave since he was out-numbered more than 20 to 1. It took Santa Anna 13 days to capture the Alamo, killing every man inside. More than 1,500 Mexican soldiers died in the assault, weakening Santa Anna's army and buying the main Texan army time.

When the two warring armies met six weeks later at the Battle of San Jacinto, Texans were furious at Santa Anna because of the Alamo, and because Santa Anna executed more than 300 Texan prisoners at Goliad shortly afterwards. Texan rebels under General Sam Houston charged into battle shouting, "Remember the Alamo!" Santa Anna was captured in the 18-minute battle, and Texas gained its independence.

FIGHTING FOR TEXAS

A. **Because Mexicans considered settlers from the U.S. trespassers on Mexican land. Texans, on the other hand, saw the conflict as a war for independence.**

11

If I remember my history class, Mexicans weren't the first people to settle Texas. The Spanish were there before them, right?

That's right, Merideth. But Native Americans were there even earlier. They first arrived in Texas about 10,000 years ago. When Spanish explorers came in the early 1500s, they found about 50 tribes. There were Pueblo tribes in the desert, and the Commanches, Apaches and others living off the enormous buffalo herds that roamed the Great Plains. One of the more advanced tribes was the Caddo in eastern Texas. They lived in large wooden buildings and grew orchards. Caddo Indians called each other "taysha," which meant "friend." The Spanish adapted the word as "Tejas," which then became "Texas."

Q. Are there any of the original Native American tribes left in Texas?

Is that why Texans are so friendly?

Well, the state motto is "Friendship," though relations between Native American Indians and settlers were hardly friendly. Spanish explorers came to Texas looking for gold. When Indians told them there was none, some Spaniards thought the Indians were lying, so they killed them. The Indians quickly learned it was better to say there *was* gold—but it was somewhere else, far away. As a result, bands of Spanish explorers wandered throughout Texas looking for gold that wasn't there. Finally, the explorers gave up. Spanish priests came to

Texas from Mexico starting in 1682 to build missions and try to convince Native Americans to convert to Christianity. These settlements encouraged other colonists from Mexico to move to Texas and start cattle ranches.

 A. **None survived the disease and fighting that came with the settlers. The Native Americans in Texas today are originally from other parts of the United States.**

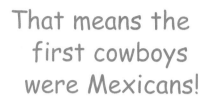 

That means the first cowboys were Mexicans!

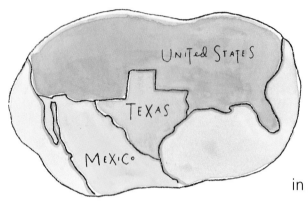

REPUBLIC OF TEXAS

You bet. Texas was part of Mexico longer than it has been part of the United States. Settlers from the United States didn't arrive in Texas until the early 1800s, and they didn't care much for Mexican rule. Mexico outlawed slavery, which was legal in America at the time. If you were not Catholic, it was difficult to own land. Most American settlers were Protestant and many wanted slaves to run cotton plantations. Plus, the language was different. These settlers had more in common with the United States than with Mexico, so they rebelled. After the Battle of San Jacinto, Texas became an independent nation. It took nine years before the United States admitted Texas into the Union. That's why Texas is known as the "Lone Star State"—it was once a one-state nation.

Q. Why did the Indians call the San Antonio River "drunken old man going home at night"?

14

What happened to the Mexicans?

Many Mexicans still come to Texas to visit and live, especially here in San Antonio and southern Texas. More than one in four Texans have a Mexican relative in their family tree. Here in San Antonio, 60 percent of the residents come from Spanish-speaking families. The colonial Spanish architecture, including the original five Spanish missions, makes it a beautiful city. Most people don't know how important San Antonio has become. With more than 1.1 million people, it is the eighth largest city in the United States. Its most famous feature is the mile-long River Walk, a beautiful district of shops, hotels and cafés lining a canal off the San Antonio River, which also has music and crowds of visitors.

THE RiverWALK

 Because there are so many twists and turns in it!

The food here sure is delicious, Tex.

The best! Mexico continues to influence our lives, from the food we eat to the language we speak. Meals like chili, tacos, enchiladas and tamales all came from this area.

Mexicans mixed the ingredients they could grow in the dry heat here, such as chili peppers, tomatoes and onions, with Texas beef to create Mexican cuisine. Hundreds of words in our language come from Spanish-speaking Mexicans who lived in Texas, including "lasso," "corral," "canyon," "plaza," "bronco," "stampede," and "buckaroo." Ironically, even though Mexicans in South Texas have enriched our food and language, this is the poorest region in Texas.

HOT! HOT! HOT!

President Lyndon B. Johnson's first job was teaching poor Mexican Americans. He was shocked by the bad conditions in which his students lived, and he vowed to

Q. Who was the first person to use the word "gobbledygook"?

help minorities and the poor. He entered politics and was elected to the U. S. Senate in 1948 by a margin of only 87 votes.

Is that why they called him "Landslide Lyndon"?

That's right, Merideth—as a joke. Johnson became known as the best senate majority leader in American history because he was very good at making people cooperate. "Come let us reason together," he would tell the other senators. In 1963, Johnson became president. He made major changes in government. He started the "Great Society" program. Laws were passed giving rights to minorities and guaranteeing blacks the right to vote. He started a "war on poverty," which included programs to help the poor, the elderly and the sick.

PRESIDENT JOHNSON BEING SWORN IN

 A. Texan Congressman Maury Maverick invented it in 1944 when he told his staff to stop using "so much gobbledygook" in their letters.

Now we're going to go up the Rio Grande.

Wow! That's one big river.

That's why they named it the "Rio Grande." It means "big river" in Spanish, (although Mexicans call it the Río Bravo). The entire Texan border with Mexico is along the Rio Grande. The river winds its way from the Rocky Mountains down into the Gulf of Mexico. The Rio Grande Valley in southernmost Texas is a warm, humid region where thousands of farmers grow onions, cucumbers, tomatoes, carrots, broccoli, lettuce, oranges and beautiful flowers. Farther north is Laredo, an important city for the booming trade between the United States and Mexico.

Q. Where was the last battle of the Civil War fought?

18

It almost feels like we are in Mexico, Tex.

¿Como Estás?

I'm Fine, You?

Nine out of ten people in Laredo are Hispanic. Almost everyone can speak both Spanish and English. Sometimes they intermingle the two languages in something called "Spanglish." Remember when I said Texas was its own country for a while? Well, when Texas became a state in 1845, Mexico refused to accept the region north of the Rio Grande as part of Texas. They even went so far as to fight a war over it—the Mexican War. When the United States won, the Rio Grande became the national border. Even today—150 years later—it is still a controversial place. Many Mexicans come across the Rio Grande in the United States illegally to work and live.

 In Brownsville, Texas, at the mouth of the Rio Grande — one month after the war had ended! Without telephones, it took a long time for news to reach Texas.

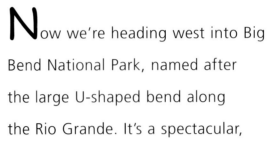

BIG BEND NATIONAL PARK

Now we're heading west into Big Bend National Park, named after the large U-shaped bend along the Rio Grande. It's a spectacular, exotic natural paradise with plunging cliffs in the Chisos Mountains and barren wasteland in the Chihuahuan Desert. There are so many giant rocks and boulders in Big Bend that Native Americans believed the Great Spirit dumped his leftover rocks there when he was finished making the world. The Rio Grande cuts through the desert, creating a green ribbon of trees, flowers and wildlife. It's a beautiful place to go rafting.

What about the animals?

Texas has the strangest critters in the country, Merideth, and some of the oddest reside right here. You'll find roadrunners scurrying through the desert. They don't fly, but they can run 20 miles per hour.

Q. What is the ugliest state animal in the nation?

20

Just like in the cartoon, they go "Beep! Beep!" and coyotes try to eat them. More than 450 bird species have been seen at Big Bend, as well as 1,000 types of plants, 115 different butterflies, and 56 reptiles and amphibians—including the Couch's Spadefoot toad, one of the few amphibians that can survive in the desert. The mosquito fish is so rare that its entire population lives in one pond in Big Bend. You'll also find antelopes, mountain lions, bears and alligators.

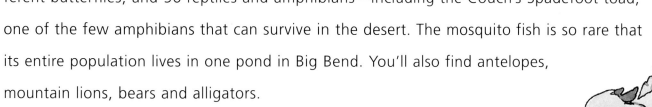

What about armadillos, Tex?

They are the oddest of all. The bony-plated armadillo is the size of a house cat and can run as fast as humans. But they cannot hear or see well. They rely mostly on their keen sense of smell to find insects in the soil for food. During the Great Depression in the 1930s, some Texans were so hungry they ate armadillos as a substitute for pork.

 A. Probably the horned toad, Texas's official state reptile. It squirts blood from its eyes when cornered!

When you're in West Texas, you're in Hollywood's Texas—the Texas of wide-open spaces, steep canyons and dried out riverbeds. This is where rugged Texan cowpokes wear spurs and look at the sun to see what time it is. It is a hot corner of Texas with temperatures routinely soaring past 100 degrees in the summer and nothing much to do. Parts of West Texas are so remote, people have to drive 100 miles to buy a pizza or a pair of shoes. There are entire counties with more square miles than people. One county, Loving County, is the most sparsely populated county in the nation.

But isn't El Paso in West Texas?

Q. Who is the Academy Awards' "Oscar" statue named after?

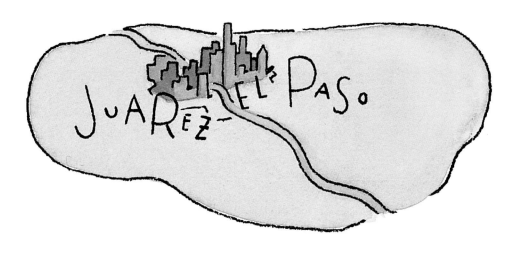

It sure is, Merideth. Perched way out on Texas's western tip, El Paso sits nestled in the Franklin Mountains along the Rio Grande. El Paso's metropolitan community spills across the Rio Grande to the Mexican city of Juárez. There are almost 2.5 million people in the two cities, making it the largest binational metropolis in the world.

El Paso is not only big, it's also old. Spanish priests and Tigua Indians built their first Texan mission at Yselta del Sur Pueblo in 1682 in El Paso after they fled a Pueblo attack in New Mexico. The Tigua have held onto their group identity in Texas, and are famous today for their arts and crafts.

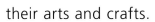

UNCLE OSCAR— IS THAT YOU?

 A Texan named Oscar Pierce. Supposedly, when his niece saw the gold figure, she said, "That looks like my uncle Oscar!"

23

Where to next, Tex?

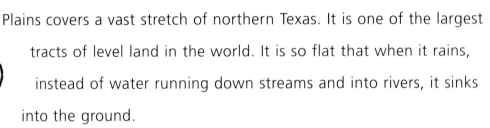

To the High Plains of North Texas, where the land is about as flat as flat can be and the weather is as violent as weather can be. The High Plains covers a vast stretch of northern Texas. It is one of the largest tracts of level land in the world. It is so flat that when it rains, instead of water running down streams and into rivers, it sinks into the ground.

On the other hand, the sky is a festival of turbulence, one of the most active weather zones in the world. Hail, dust storms, strong winds and snow are an almost constant part of life in the High Plains, which is why it is called "Tornado Alley." More than 100 twisters a year sweep through the High Plains, packing winds of 250 miles per hour—strong enough to lift a tractor-trailer truck off the highway and fling it through the air like a rag doll.

Q. What special monument can you find in Groom, Texas?

Texas has some of the most extreme weather phenomena in the nation. A winter storm once dumped five feet of snow in the town of Vega. On August 4, 1979, 29 inches of rain fell in Albany, Texas—all that in one day! On the other hand, some parts of Texas get almost no rain at all.

And it's not just the weather. Texas accounts for six percent of the world's meteor activity, more than any other state. Eighty meteors have been recorded hitting Texas.

A famous Civil War general, Philip Sheridan, thought Texas weather and landscape were so bleak, he said, "If I owned both Hell and Texas, I'd rent out Texas and live in Hell."

He was kidding, of course.

I don't know. He was a Yankee, after all!

A. The largest cross in the Western Hemisphere. It is 190 feet tall!

The High Plains was the last part of Texas to be settled. Giant herds of buffalo once roamed the range, and Indian tribes hunted them for survival. After the Civil War in the 1860s, the military stepped up its campaign to wipe out the Native Americans. To eliminate the tribes' source of food, hunting parties went into the Plains and killed hundreds of thousands of buffalo. By 1880, the herds and Native Americans were gone.

That sounds terrible.

It was a brutal time, Merideth. Ranchers moved in and this became cattle country. Wide open spaces and warm weather make Texas a great place for cattle, which was why the first Spanish settlers built ranches, and American settlers kept on raising more cattle. By 1860, there were six cows for every person in Texas. After the Civil War, cattle helped rebuild Texas after it been defeated along with

Q. **What's the Texas Panhandle?**

the rest of the South. Cows ran wild, and lawlessness prevailed in parts of Texas. The government allowed Texans to round up whatever cattle they could find. They moved the cattle in giant drives of longhorn steers crisscrossing the state. The invention of barbed wire brought fences to Texas, ending the short but romantic era of roundups on the open range. It is still cattle country, but the cattle drives are long gone.

CATTLE DRIVE

What's a longhorn steer?

Mexican ranchers bred longhorns to live off of the range. Just like in the movies, cowboys would herd them together and guide them to market towns or railroad junctions to be slaughtered for meat. Their long horns may look scary, but they would rarely try to hurt a person.

A. The Panhandle, in northwestern Texas, got its name because the region is shaped like the handle of a pan connected to the rest of the state.

27

What happened to the longhorns?

There are hardly any left. They were good for grazing on the range, not in fenced ranches. But Texas is still famous for its beef cattle. With more than 15 million cows, there are almost as many cattle as there are people. The state's largest cattle auction is held weekly in Amarillo in the center of the Panhandle. More than 100,000 cattle change hands every Tuesday.

What about all the Texas barbecues?

Texas barbecues go back to the days of the open range. Cowboys butchered a steer and cooked the best parts over an open fire. Seems like every town and city in Texas claims to serve "the best barbecue in Texas." In Amarillo, one restaurant offers a 72-ounce steak free—as long as you can eat it in an hour.

Q. **Where does the word "maverick" come from?**

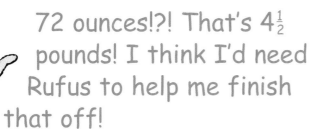

72 ounces!?! That's $4\frac{1}{2}$ pounds! I think I'd need Rufus to help me finish that off!

Amarillo is a quirky place, Merideth. Local businessmen commissioned artists in 1974 to bury 10 Cadillacs in a wheat field along Route 66, with their back ends popping up from the ground at a 52-degree angle (the same angle as the Great Pyramid in Egypt). The businessmen called it a salute to the American automobile, and "Cadillac Ranch" has become one of Texas's best-known attractions. There are also more than 3,000 road signs with everything from images of Marilyn Monroe to gibberish. Amarillo even has an $8\frac{1}{2}$-ton stainless-steel monument dedicated to helium, which used to be big business locally.

Amarillo is also the headquarters for the world's largest horse registry. It's one of Texas's last big cowboy towns.

CADILLAC RANCH

A. When Samuel A. Maverick refused to brand his cattle, unbranded cows were called "mavericks." Today, the word describes folks who don't go along with everyone else.

29

Now, on to the Hill Country in Central Texas. It is one of the most attractive parts of Texas, and we can learn more about cowboys there. Located north of San Antonio and west of Austin, the region serves as a natural playground with parks, lush valleys, swimming holes and rivers loaded with bass. There are some very special places here. My favorite is the Enchanted Rock State Park. It got its name because of a 400-foot-high cliff made of pinkish rock that supposedly used to make noises. Native Americans believed the sounds came from gods whispering. Scientists think the noises were simply the rock settling as the weather and temperatures changed.

Shhh.

Cool! But what about the cowboys?

This area used to be cowboy country. One town, Bandera, claims to be the cowboy capital of Texas.

Q. **Who was Judge Roy Bean?**

The Cowboy Artists of
America Museum is in Kerrville.

The image of cowboys as glamorous figures came
from artists, writers and, later, filmmakers, who portrayed them as heroic men on the
frontier. But many of the artists and writers never even saw real cowboys. If they had,
they would have learned that being a cowboy was really hard, dangerous work. Even
when cowboys were in their heyday after the Civil War, there were only
10,000 to 20,000 of them in Texas, many of whom were ex-slaves,

Mexican Americans and former Confederate soldiers.
It was a rootin'-tootin' time, but it wasn't a lifestyle
that most people wanted to live.

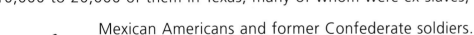

 He was one of Texas's most notorious judges during the cowboy era. He ran his court out of a bar and sometimes staged prizefights between convicts.

But what about you, Tex?
Aren't you a cowboy? You
sure look and sound like one.

BEEP

MoDern Texas

Heck no. Like most Texans, I've never
even been on a horse. My parents work at the University of
Texas in Austin. Their ancestors moved here from
Czechoslovakia 150 years ago to be cotton farmers.
When I grow up, I want to program computers—
that's where the future is in Texas. The closest I've gotten to
bustin' a bronco is going to the rodeo, the official sport of Texas.

What exactly is a rodeo?

"Rodeo" means "roundup" in Spanish. Rodeos date back to the 1700s when
cowboys used to perform tricks as entertainment. When barbed wire closed the open
ranges, the roundups stopped. But people still wanted to see cowboys perform their
tricks. Almost every large town and city holds rodeos today. Modern-day rodeos include

Q. What almost started a war between Texas
and France in the 1830s?

calf roping, livestock shows, riding contests, bucking broncos and more.

Well, can you take me to your hometown of Austin?

Sure thing, Merideth. It's a great city.

Austin is the capital of Texas, and was named after Stephen F. Austin, the "Father of Texas." When Austin was a young man in the 1820s, he convinced Mexico to provide land for settlers from the United States, and arranged for more than 6,000 Americans to move to Texas. When the U.S. settlers and Mexican authorities started to feud, he tried to intervene. But the Mexican government arrested Austin and accused him of trying to start a revolution. He later returned to Texas after it became an independent country.

 Pigs! War was almost declared after roving groups of pigs entered the French embassy and ate beds and important papers.

33

Why are we hanging out at this bridge, Tex?

This is my favorite place in Austin, Merideth, and we're not the ones "hanging out." More than a million Mexican free-tailed bats hang from the cracks, rafters and crevices under Congress Avenue Bridge. Every sunset they fly out from under the bridge. It is a spectacular sight.

Yikes!

Don't complain. They eat more than 20,000 pounds of insects every night. That's a lot of bugs! Let's go to Barton Springs Pool, a much cleaner natural wonder. This 1,000-foot-long natural spring pool is as clear as crystal and serves as the city's swimming hole. Thousands of residents and

Q. How many different national flags have flown over Texas?

students from the University of Texas gather here to cool off, catch some rays, and just have fun with their friends.

But what about tourists?

There's the Texas State Capitol Building, the seventh-largest government building in the world. It measures 311 feet from the basement floor to the crown of the Goddess of Liberty statue atop the dome. That's as high as a 30-story building. It cost so much money to build it in the 1880s, the state sold 3 million acres across 10 counties in the High Plains to a Chicago company to pay for it. Called XIT (as in "Ten in Texas"), it was the largest ranch in Texas until it was broken up into small plots for farmers. Today, Texas's largest ranch is King Ranch, a 1.2 million acre lot almost the size of Delaware. It's produced cotton, cattle, oil and a horse that won the Triple Crown.

 Six. France, Spain, Mexico, the Republic of Texas, the United States, and the Confederate States of America have all claimed sovereignty over Texas.

35

What's that rocking beat I hear?

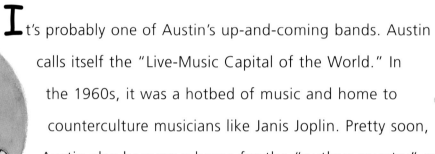

It's probably one of Austin's up-and-coming bands. Austin calls itself the "Live-Music Capital of the World." In the 1960s, it was a hotbed of music and home to counterculture musicians like Janis Joplin. Pretty soon, Austin also became a home for the "outlaw country" music movement, led by Willie Nelson. Today, with the University of Texas and the booming technology industry here, Austin is still a hip music town—but a successful business town, too.

I didn't know Texas was famous for its music.

Q. Has Austin always been the capital of Texas?

Texas musicians have influenced American music more than any other state! Texas was the home of the blues, starting with singers like Blind Lemon Jefferson (yes, he was really blind) in the 1920s going right up to BB King

BuDDy HoLLy

today. Buddy Holly hailed from the High Plains where he practically invented rock 'n' roll. We can't take credit for starting country and western music, but believe me—it's everywhere in Texas, and it's good! Now there's the Tejano music movement, a blend of Mexican and Texan sounds that's been around since the 1800s. And it isn't just popular music. Some of the best symphonies in the country are in Texas. Every four years, musicians compete at the Van Cliburn Piano Competition. It's held in Fort Worth and that's where we're headed next.

A. No. Texas's capital has changed seven times, more than any other state.

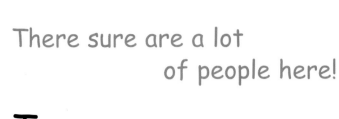

There sure are a lot
of people here!

The Dallas-Fort Worth area is the fastest-growing region in Texas, with more than 5 million people. (There are 20 million Texans altogether, more people than any other state except California.) Texas grew by 3 million people in the 1990s, or by as many people as in the entire state of Oregon.

People say that "Dallas is where the East peters out; Fort Worth is where the West begins." Fort Worth's nickname, "Cowtown," dates back to the days when cowboys herded millions of cattle here as the end point of the Chisolm Trail. It was a rough place. One notorious section of town was called Hell's Half Acre, where bandits like Butch Cassidy and the Sundance Kid spent their time.

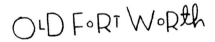

OLD FORT WORTH

But what about those famous
lawmen, the Texas Rangers?

Q. Who's the most famous Texas Ranger to never carry a gun?

John C. Hays formed the Texas Rangers in 1840, four years after Texas became an independent country. Armed with six-shooters and a saddle gun, they fought Indians, Mexican bands that raided Texas, and a wide assortment of horse thieves, murderers, and other lawbreakers, including the famous Texan bank robbers Clyde Barrow and Bonnie Parker—commonly known as "Bonnie and Clyde"—in the 1930s.

Texas Rangers never wore a uniform or saluted each other, but folks said they could be recognized by their hard work and toughness. Their motto was "One riot, one Ranger."

TEXAS RANGER ON THE TRAIL OF BONNIE AND CLYDE

In 1935, the Texas Legislature created the Texas Department of Public Safety, and the Rangers became part of that agency. The Rangers' legend lives on at the Texas Rangers Hall of Fame and Museum in Waco with lots of saddles, guns and heroic tales.

A. **Nolan Ryan was a pitcher for the Texas Rangers and the Houston Astros. A Texan himself, Ryan holds the major league record for throwing 5,714 strike-outs.**

39

But what about Dallas, Tex?

First, the fun stuff. The first convenience store in the country, a 7-Eleven, opened in Dallas on July 11, 1927. In 1958, a Texas Instruments engineer named Jack Kilby invented the microchip in Dallas. Mary Kay began her door-to-door cosmetics business from Dallas in 1963. The company now has more than 300,000 beauty consultants going door-to-door all over the world.

And the Dallas Cowboys?

That's the name of the famous football team with all the pretty cheerleaders. In fact, Dallas was never really a cowboy town; it was first built by cotton farmers. The region's rich soil made it one of the most important cotton-growing regions in the nation. That's why they hold the Cotton Bowl college football game here every year.

Q. How did Dallas get its name?

So what isn't fun?

TEXAS SCHOOL BOOK
DEPOSITORY BUILDING

On November 22, 1963, President John F. Kennedy was in an open car waving to crowds in Dallas when three shots rang out, killing Kennedy and wounding Texas Governor John Connally. It was the worst day in Dallas's history. Police arrested Lee Harvey Oswald and accused him of shooting Kennedy from the sixth floor of the Texas School Book Depository Building. You can learn all about it at the Sixth Floor Museum in Dallas, located on the very spot where Oswald fired the fatal shot. It's an important, if terrible, part of our history.

A. Dallas is named after Vice President George Mifflin Dallas of Pennsylvania who supported Texas statehood in the 1840s.

So Dallas was a cotton town. But how about the rest of the state?

Money from oil helped build much of the rest of Texas. In 1901, two drillers named Patillo Higgins and Anthony Lucas punched a hole in an underground salt dome at a place called Spindletop in eastern Texas. Oil gushed out, soaring higher than a 20-story building. That's when the oil boom hit Texas. Thousands of drillers dug deep into the ground searching for "black gold," named because of oil's color and (occasionally) high value. Out of the scramble, huge and important companies emerged like Exxon, Texaco and Chevron.

Later discoveries in and around Texas helped fuel the economy, which rose and fell with oil. During the good times, oil money went into real estate, banks, technology and factories. But oil hasn't always brought wealth to Texas. In the 1930s, drillers were producing much more oil than people wanted to use. The price dropped to a couple of pennies a barrel. Instead of getting rich, some Texan oilmen went bankrupt.

Q. How much crude oil does Texas produce per year?

Was Houston built on oil, Tex?

It sure was, Merideth. Houston today is a huge center for the oil industry with oil refineries, petrochemical manufacturers, and a gigantic harbor. Spindletop helped nearby Houston, which had been a sleepy little town on a swamp at the edge of Galveston Bay. But Houston is on a swamp, and it is a very hot, muggy place. The average summertime temperature is 94 degrees. It was not a pleasant place to live—that is, until air conditioning was invented in the 1930s. That's around the time Houston really took off. It went from 100,000 residents to a million in 20 years. Today, more energy is spent on air conditioning in Houston than on every light and appliance in the city.

 650 million barrels—more than any other state—despite the fact that an 1899 geological survey noted that there was "little or no chance for oil ... in Texas!"

What else is in Houston besides oil?

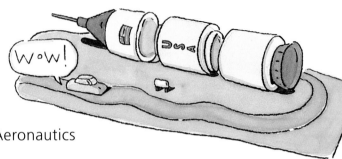

Lots of stuff, Merideth. Probably the most famous is the Johnson Space Center. The National Aeronautics and Space Administration (NASA) uses the center to direct all manned space missions and to train astronauts, conduct space research, and build space equipment. Some of the spaceships are on display. But Houston isn't only about rocket science. The nation's largest annual cattle show and second largest rodeo are held in Houston. Then there's the Astrodome. Built in 1966, the 66,000-seat, air-conditioned indoor stadium was billed as "the world's eighth wonder." "Astroturf" was invented for the stadium as a substitute for grass.

How did Houston get its name?

After Sam Houston, the victorious general at the Battle of San Jacinto, the first president of Texas, and the first U.S. senator from

Q. What famous dinosaur came from Texas?

Texas. One time Sam Houston went against Texas, however, was during the Civil War. He opposed his beloved state's decision to join the Confederacy in 1861.

How about heroic women from Texas?

There's been plenty of them—Ma Ferguson, for one. Miriam Amanda "Ma" Ferguson was the first woman elected governor of Texas, and the second woman governor in the United States. She became governor in 1925 after her husband was impeached. Ma Ferguson's main issues as governor were helping poor farmers and opposing the Ku Klux Klan, a racist organization that was very powerful in Texas. More recently there was Barbara Jordan, one of the first African-American women to enter national politics. She grew up in Houston and was the first woman and black person to be elected to Congress from Texas. She became famous in 1974 when Congress debated whether to impeach President Richard Nixon. "I have finally been included in 'We, the People,'" Jordan said, referring to the opening words of the Constitution. "My faith in the Constitution is whole, it is complete, it is total."

A. Barney! Texan Sheryl Leach created the purple television dinosaur after she couldn't find a good video for her son to watch.

Alright, Merideth, here we are at our last stop—the Gulf Coastal Plain, scene of Texas's greatest glory and fury. First the glory. At the Battle of Sabine Pass in 1863, 44 Texans with 6 cannons held off a fleet of 4 Union gunships, 22 other boats and 5,000 soldiers. They even captured 400 Yankees! The Texans received the only Confederate medals awarded for bravery during the entire Civil War. That's one example of Texan courage. Another was Audie Murphy of Farmersville, Texas—the most decorated American soldier in World War II. In one battle, Murphy fought off 250 German soldiers by himself.

Remind me never to pick a fight with a Texan! What about the fury?

On September 8, 1900, a hurricane blew into Galveston, submerging the once bustling port city of 37,000 people under 20 feet of water. More than 6,000 people were killed. It was the worst natural disaster in the history of the United States. A ten-mile sea wall was built afterwards to protect the city from another hurricane, but Galveston never regained its status as a major port.

Q. **What was the first word broadcast to Earth from the moon?**

Texas's coast stretches from Louisiana to the Mexican border. Farmers grow cotton, oranges, tomatoes, vegetables, rice, watermelons and other crops in its rich soil. A 432-mile waterway, called "the Big Ditch," makes it easy to haul products behind the chain of barrier islands that protect Texas's mainland from the rough Gulf of Mexico waters. Some of the islands are beautiful and fun. The long, white-sand beaches are perfect for swimming and sand castles. The Padre Island National Seashore in the south is the longest barrier island in the world and a great place to see wildlife.

So that's it. Texas in a nutshell. What did you think?

Incredible—mountains in West Texas, the beach in the east, and all kinds of stuff in between! Rufus and I had no idea that Texas has so much to see, do and learn about. Thanks a lot, Tex. We had a blast!

 A. **"Houston." On June 20, 1969, Neil Armstrong radioed Mission Control. "Houston," he said, "the eagle has landed."**

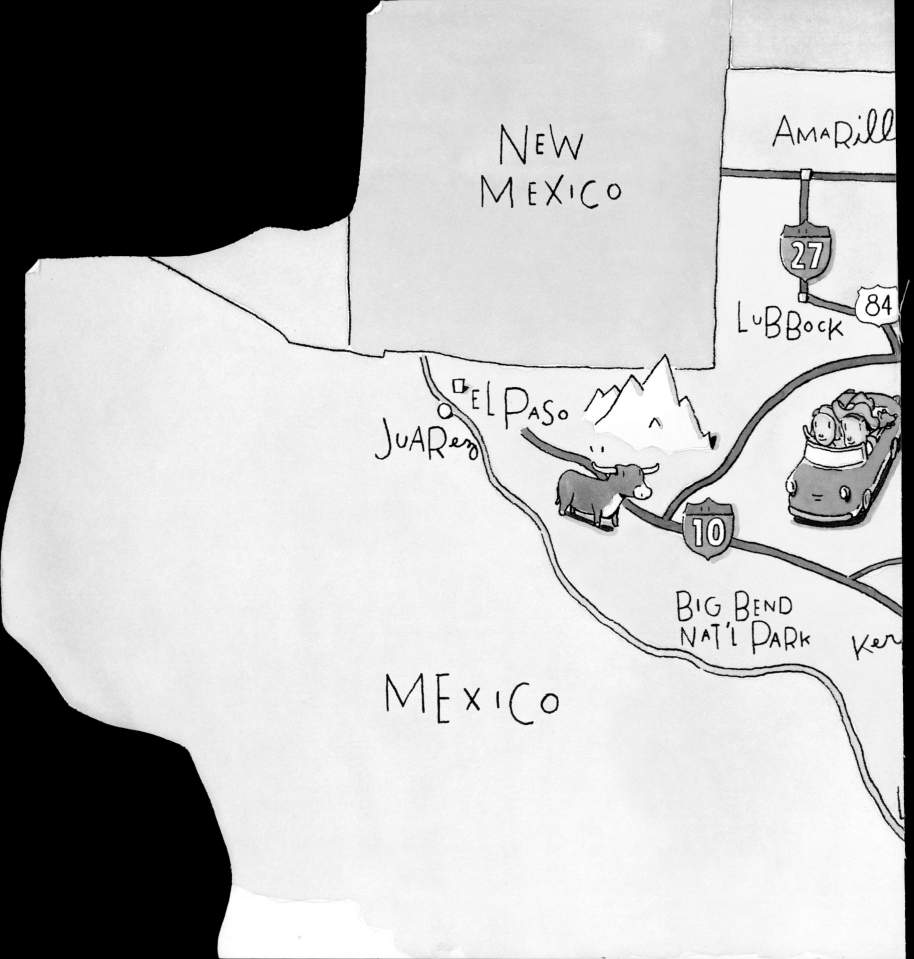

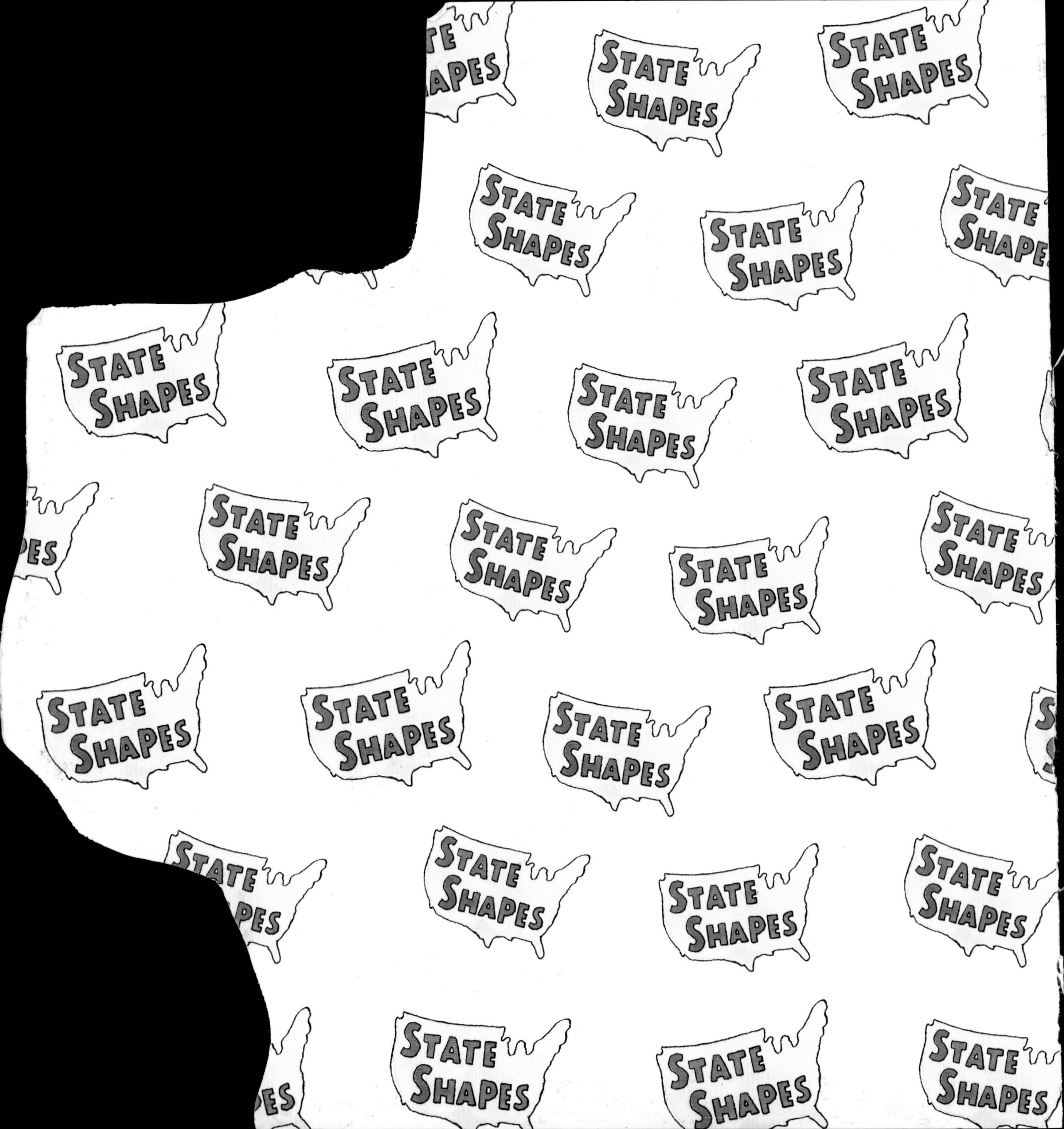
STATE SHAPES